Healing Addictive Behavior
Yogic Science for Transformation
as taught by Yogi Bhajan®

Mukta Kaur Khalsa, Ph.D.

ISBN 978-0-9799192-5-1

Layout and Design by I Was There Press
PO Box 10210 Fairbanks, AK 99710
www.birchtreedesigns.net/publishing.html

SUPERHEALTH® IS AN AFFILIATE OF 3HO FOUNDATION
www.super-health.net

To request permission, please write to:
SuperHealth®, Inc. 1A Ram Das Guru Place Española, NM 87532
superhealth12@gmail.com
And to:
KRI PO Box 1819 Santa Cruz, NM 87567
www.kriteachings.org

Mukta Kaur Khalsa, Ph.D.
Editorial and research support graciously provided by Jocelyn Suchas Johnson, Nirinjan Kaur, Gurumeet Kaur Khalsa, Rampreet Kaur.

Printed by Pettit Network Inc.
3070 Pike Avenue South, Afton, MN 55001
www.pettitnetwork.com

Distributed by Itasca Books
www.itascabooks.com

Healing Addictive Behavior
Yogic Science for Transformation
as taught by Yogi Bhajan®

Mukta Kaur Khalsa, Ph.D.

I WAS THERE PRESS

Dedication

This book is dedicated to my beloved teacher, Yogi Bhajan. He came to the West and taught timeless yogic teachings that are effective for dealing with the issues facing contemporary society. This book is lovingly presented in the name of his legacy.

May it touch the heart and exalt the spirit
giving hope for a new day.

Acknowledgments

I wish to personally express my sincere and heartfelt gratitude for the support we have received. It has been a consolidated effort to produce this book.

A very special thank you to Jocelyn Suchas Johnson, Nirinjan Kaur, Gurumeet Kaur Khalsa, Fateh Singh and Rampreet Kaur for their dedicated service and invaluable skills. Without their contributions this book may not have been produced.

May our prayer be heard as one voice, one strength, and one conscious effort to uplift humanity.

Mukta Kaur Khalsa, Ph.D.

How To Use This Book

This book offers a unique approach to overcoming substance abuse and other dependencies. It is a compilation of authentic teachings from Yogi Bhajan for changing habitual behavior. This yogic system is priceless.

This first series focuses on SuperHealth® protocols for dealing with alcohol, nicotine, marijuana and cocaine. The SuperHealth® technology is precise and effective. It can be used practically in your life today or under the guidance of a licensed health practitioner.

In these rapidly changing times there is tremendous stress upon the human sensory system. According to Yogi Bhajan this causes "Information Dementia Syndrome," an overload of information bombarding the psyche. To relieve the pressure one can easily turn to stimulants or depressants just to "get by." A habit can be formed, and over time, lead to an addiction. From the SuperHealth® perspective, this temporary coping mechanism compensates for a lack of inner fulfillment and vitality. The use of drugs, alcohol, overeating, unhealthy relationships and other behaviors can give momentary satisfaction, but can never replace the inner peace, confidence and self-control that come from a connection to our *True Self*.

Some of this information is published for the first time. Share it freely with your family, friends and colleagues. May it lead to greater happiness, health and prosperity!

Medical Disclaimer

The information and nutritional formulas contained in this book are not a substitute for medical care or treatment. This is an educational guide designed to teach the use of Kundalini Yoga and meditation to support your health and well-being. SuperHealth® encourages abstinence from alcohol and the non-clinical use of drugs. Combining Kundalini Yoga with alcohol or drugs may be harmful to your health.

Anyone with a reason to suspect illness should seek licensed medical advice and care. Over the years many people have received benefits from the underlying principles of detoxifying through diet. We make every effort to provide up-to-date information intended to be integrated with, not replace, the advice of a licensed medical professional.

Professional Advancement

SuperHealth® is an approved Education and Training Provider for CEUs (Continuing Education Units) by:

- NAADAC for addiction professionals, counselors and behavioral health specialists by the National Certification Commission.
- State of California Board of Sciences for MFTs and LCSWs.

These ancient and therapeutic formulas can complement traditional treatment regimens by:

- Improving function of blood chemistry, food metabolism and nervous and glandular systems.

- Providing nutritional tips and foods to cleanse and rebuild body systems.

- Revitalizing and renewing energy levels and spiritual vitality.

- Supporting a healthy lifestyle to improve the quality of life.

For further information please visit: www.super-health.net

Yogi Bhajan (1929-2004)

In 1968 Yogi Bhajan came to America to teach Kundalini Yoga. At that time people in the West were seeking spiritual fulfillment. He found youth using drugs to escape the emptiness and isolation of their cultural environment. Middle class housewives were taking pills with the distorted hope that it would numb their inner unhappiness. Businessmen used alcohol to deal with the stress of everyday living.

Yogi Bhajan addressed these problems at a grass-roots level. He started teaching Kundalini Yoga and meditation classes and slowly people discovered a way of feeling good naturally. As an experiment, he housed two substance abusers in his center in Washington, D.C. For two weeks, in a 24/7 controlled environment, he implemented a treatment program based on Kundalini Yoga and meditation. An amazing thing happened to these individuals. They overcame their addiction and were changed men. This was the birth of SuperHealth®.

In 1973 SuperHealth® opened its doors in Tucson, Arizona, and offered a residential program blending the ancient formulas of the East with the innovations of the West. It developed into a systemized program with customized treatment plans for behavioral addictions including stress, substance abuse and other unhealthy habits and emotional disorders. The program included three Kundalini Yoga and meditation classes each day, a specific detoxification and rehabilitation diet complete with fresh juices, a vitamin and herbal regime, counseling and therapeutic massage.

By 1978, SuperHealth® became accredited by the prestigious Joint Commission on Accreditation of Healthcare Organizations. It became classified in the top 10% of all treatment programs throughout the United States. The precious and sacred teachings were revolutionizing the therapeutic model for the treatment of behavioral addiction.

Yogi Bhajan is one of four humanitarians to have received a Joint Congressional Resolution by the United States Congress honoring his life's work and teachings. The other recipients are Mother Teresa, Dr. Martin Luther King, Jr. and Pope John Paul II.

Yogi Bhajan passed away October 6, 2004.

Message from the Author

When I started working with Yogi Bhajan in 1973 we often met people who didn't know the difference between yoga and yogurt. In the years since, yoga has become quite mainstream, while the issues we set out to address through SuperHealth® are perhaps even more pronounced than they were back then.

We understood that with the stress of the Information Age our psyches would be bombarded and over-stimulated, creating depression, isolation, disillusion and frustration. Kundalini Yoga is the yoga of awareness and develops the full use of the brain's potential for personal experience and development.

Kundalini Yoga, meditation, nutrition formulas, recipes and therapeutic juice blends can expedite the healing process and harmoniously bring a person to a state of physical, mental and spiritual balance. It is a sacred science not only for today, but more importantly, for tomorrow.

The SuperHealth® Way

SuperHealth® is a highly effective approach to help you reach your highest potential. It is for anyone who wants to succeed in facing life's tidal wave of challenges with happiness, health and prosperity.

The system is based on ancient yogic science that can effectively deal with modern-day habits involving drugs, alcohol, food, smoking, codependency, depression, stress, gambling, and many other behaviors. The neurons of the brain must be changed to alter patterns of addictive behavior. A person only adjusts behavior and sustains the change when their awareness or consciousness has been heightened.

Practices such as Kundalini Yoga and meditation can facilitate greater awareness of the self, the environment and an internal belief system.

Toxic substances break down the nervous system. When functioning properly, a strong nervous system supports the ability to meet life's challenges with inner strength, determination and "grit." The glandular system is the guardian of health, but it too becomes compromised during toxic build-up.

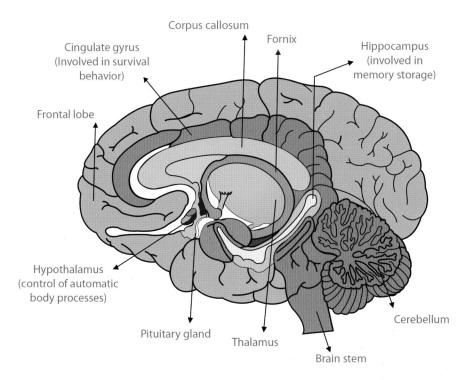

Corpus callosum

Cingulate gyrus
(Involved in survival
behavior)

Fornix

Hippocampus
(involved in
memory storage)

Frontal lobe

Hypothalamus
(control of automatic
body processes)

Pituitary gland

Thalamus

Brain stem

Cerebellum

Impact of Toxic Substances

The following are some general effects of toxic build-up in
the body:

- Damages brain cells and limits the brain's ability to
regulate and produce neurotransmitters.

- Triggers an imbalance in the glandular system,
compromising optimal health.

- Weakens the nervous system, limiting the ability to
maintain self-control and mental clarity.

- Causes malnutrition as toxins interfere with the
brain's ability to regulate nutritional needs.

Components of SuperHealth®

SuperHealth® technology offers advanced methods known to promote a change in behavior and create a healthy and balanced presence with a consolidated state of mind.

The remainder of this chapter will discuss the following key components of SuperHealth®:

- Kundalini Yoga and Meditation as taught by Yogi Bhajan®
- Nutritional Restoration
- Science of Humanology
- Counseling

Kundalini Yoga

Kundalini Yoga as taught by Yogi Bhajan® is referred to as the yoga of awareness. In conjunction with meditation and specific detoxification and rehabilitation diets, the precision of this ancient technology restores health and vitality to a system compromised by toxic build-up.

An overtaxed nervous system can leave you more vulnerable and easily influenced by temptations, urges and cravings. The side effects are fatigue, anxiety, depression and disassociation from a spiritual connection within.

Kundalini Yoga strengthens the nervous system which is often weakened by substances, poor eating habits and stress. It changes the chemistry of the blood, regulates food metabolism and increases the functioning of the glandular, circulatory, digestive and eliminatory systems.

The practice of Kundalini Yoga helps restore and balance the sympathetic and parasympathetic nervous systems (see glossary, page 78-84) through postures and breathing techniques. This alleviates damage to the nerves caused by harmful substances.

Once these critical body systems are rebuilt and revitalized, an individual is better able to handle pressure without resorting to harmful habits that can lead to an addiction.

Meditation

Meditation addresses psychological dependence issues and promotes clarity of thought and the ability to focus, discriminate and make decisions through neutrality without reacting emotionally. Coupled with Kundalini Yoga, it provides the discipline to carry out intentions with one-pointedness of mind and fortitude of spirit. The addictive personality is thus transformed and develops the immunity to protect itself from outside pressures in a healthy way.

Kundalini Yoga and meditation techniques are beneficial to the cleansing and healing process.

To find a Kundalini Yoga center, please visit www.3HO.org or www.kriteachings.org.

The Breath

The way you breathe affects your state of mind. Specific breathing techniques have profound effects on the body and mental attitude. The breath has the ability to increase your state of awareness while enhancing vitality and health.

SuperHealth® primarily utilizes three yogic breathing techniques, each described in greater detail on pages 54-63 of this book: Long Deep Breathing, Breath of Fire and Sitali Pranayam. These three breathing techniques are used extensively to help eliminate toxins from the body.

For each of these techniques, the breath begins at the abdomen. Increased oxygen flows to the brain bringing greater awareness. These breathing techniques are an important and effective part of the SuperHealth® regimen. They promote general well-being and help to overcome mental distraction.

Many other techniques are also included in this book. Try them and experience the healing effects of the breath!

Nutritional Restoration

The cleansing and rehabilitation diets of SuperHealth® are specifically designed with therapeutic juice formulas that enrich the chemistry of the blood, regulate food metabolism and cleanse toxic overload.

The diets allow the body to quickly assimilate and eliminate food while improving digestive functioning. The healing properties of food cleanse and rebuild the body in order to restore the system to its natural state of health and well-being.

This book outlines specific foods that nourish, heal and detoxify the body.

The Science of Humanology

Humanology is applied psychology from the perspective of Kundalini Yoga. It is a system of realizing the optimal potential for success and excellence. Its practical application provides lifestyle skills that address the full spectrum of human existence, ranging from a mental attitude of self-defeat to self relliance and from generational parental phobias to compassionate parental identity. It also speaks to creative identity, projection and communication, success and prosperity, and prevention of relapse.

During the formative years of early childhood, both spoken and unspoken messages from parents and society are imprinted into the psyche and imbedded in the subconscious mind.

Strong values and self-esteem are created in a supportive, respectful and nurturing environment. If absent, an addictive personality can develop, filling the unmet needs with subconscious patterns related to haunting thoughts, memories, fears and nightmares.

Once a person becomes aware of this dynamic, change can begin. Healing is accelerated with the practice of Kundalini Yoga, meditation and a proper diet, all of which increase awareness about the way we think, eat and live.

The practical application of the Science of Humanology will be addressed more fully in the next SuperHealth® series publication.

Counseling and Self-Healing

The ultimate goal in counseling is to guide someone to their personal quietness so they know what action is best for them to take. It is not only important to *know* what to do. One must also develop the *ability* through nervous system strength to successfully follow through in this process. Practical yogic tools facilitate "inner grit," mental clarity and decisiveness for self-counseling. The technology improves the functioning of the nervous and glandular systems and enables a good decision-making process.

Developing an understanding of one's true nature empowers self-healing. This building of physical resiliency is essential to support change. Feelings of despair and emptiness associated with fears are replaced with a sense of clarity and hope. Over time, the wisdom gained from these experiences can lead to an inner strength that is an especially important tool during challenging situations. With practice, the process of change and discipline becomes natural and rewarding.

ALCOHOL

Impact of Alcohol on the Body and Mind

Affects almost every system and organ in the body, from the lungs to the sex organs.

Causes low blood sugar, hepatitis and cirrhosis, since most alcohol is metabolized by the liver.

Is a strong nervous system depressant and raises the risk of brain damage.

Prolonged intake may lead to heart rhythm problems, hypertension and heart attacks.

Increases the risk of cancer in many different organs.

Affects parts of the brain that govern:
- Judgment, inhibition
- Balance, motor coordination
- Blackouts and memory loss from high doses
- May cause permanent brain damage, stroke and dementia over long periods of time
- Thought processes and consciousness

Effects of alcohol use on the brain could include:
- Brain atrophy and shrinkage
- Slowing of processing of information from eyes, ears, mouth and other senses
- Difficulty thinking clearly, poor judgment and learning
- Exaggerated states of emotion and memory loss (Limbic System)

Affects the corpus callosum, the tissue connecting and passing information through the right and left hemispheres of the brain.

Risk of fetal exposure (Fetal Alcohol Syndrome):

- Fewer brain cells, leading to long term problems in learning, memory and behavior.
- Possibility of infants with growth deficiencies, poorly formed bones and organs, heart abnormalities.
- Studies show smoking cigarettes combined with alcohol increases chance of birth defects and miscarriage.

Affects the cerebellum, the center of movement and balance:

- Loss of coordination
- Personal injury—staggering, tripping and falling

Affects the hypothalamus and pituitary system:

- Decreases sexual performance
- Increases urination

Affects the medulla (brain stem):

- Sleepiness; loss of consciousness
- Slowing of breath and heart rate, eventually reaching fatal levels

Addictive and psychological effects:

- It is an addictive drug, inducing a high risk for abuse, dependence and alcoholism.
- Alcoholism is linked to low self-esteem, depression and isolation.
- Drinking affects work and family responsibilities, putting self at risk in dangerous situations.
- When reduced or stopped, intense symptoms of withdrawal occur, including sweating, nausea, vomiting and delirium tremens (or DTs), which involves severe shaking, confusion and anxiety. Symptoms this severe require medical detoxification before treatment.

Social Factors:

- Peer pressure —culture of usage starts at a young age.
- Advertising—advocated as safe and glamorous.

SuperHealth® Perspective on Alcohol

Alcohol interferes with the regulation of blood sugar, which is controlled in the area behind the pineal gland in the hypothalamus.

This area may be balanced during the detoxification phase with therapeutic juice blends and vitamins coupled with using specific meditations. During this detoxification process the functioning of the glandular system shows significant improvement.

This specific regimen can make alcohol taste repellent, similar to a natural antabuse.

Three Stages of Intervention

Light Stage: Practice of Kundalini Yoga and use of therapeutic nutritional formulas will benefit a light stage drinker.

More Degenerative: Because of physical dependence and low stamina for exercise, a cleansing regimen is recommended. The need to medically detoxify must be considered and discussed with your doctor. After medical detoxification, eat a nutritous diet, including fresh fruits and vegetables, whole grains, nuts, seeds and foods that are light, organic and easily digestable.

Very Degenerative: Dependence requires medical detoxification and supervision when there is the possibility of withdrawal symptoms including seizures, convulsions and delirium tremens. After medical detoxification, rebuild the system with a specific rehabilitation regimen consisting of Kundalini Yoga and the restorative therapeutic nutritional formulas and cleansing diet.

Kundalini Yoga Exercises & Meditations to Promote Healing from the Effects of Alcohol

See pages 52-64 for pose instructions.

Habituation Meditation   *page 63*

This is one of the best meditations for any type of dependence and specifically benefits drug rehabilitation by supporting the formation of new constructive habits and behaviors.

Sitali Pranayam   *page 56*

Sitali Pranayam enhances power, strength, and vitality. It has a cooling, calming and cleansing effect. Initially, the tongue may taste bitter (a sign of detoxification), and eventually may become sweet tasting.

Breath of Fire   *page 55*

Breath of Fire will help the functioning of the pituitary gland which regulates the entire glandular system. This will restore nervous system strength to cleanse and renew the blood. Begin with 3 minutes, then work up to 5 minutes, 11 minutes and eventually 31 minutes daily.

Cow Pose Pumps   *page 58*

Cow Pose Pumps increase energy and improve digestion. Doing this exercise helps release blockage from toxins stored in the back of the neck which impact short-term memory. Eventually, when practiced regularly, this exercise helps eliminate these substances from the system.

Sat Kriya

Sat Kriya   *page 53*

Sat Kriya is one of the most beneficial Kundalini Yoga kriyas. It improves overall general physical health, strengthens the entire system and stimulates its natural flow of energy. This exercise helps to reduce sexual phobias.

Therapeutic Nutritional Formulas

See pages 66-76 for recipes.

Celery Juice

Strengthens the nervous system and has a calming and soothing effect.

- Drink one 8 oz. glass up to 3 times a day. A glass before bed is recommended, especially for insomnia.

Grapefruit Juice

Diuretic; aids in elimination.

- Drink one 8 oz. glass 3 times throughout the day.

Carrot and Celery Juice

Improves function of the liver and strengthens the nervous system.

- Drink every 2 hours, alternating ratios: 1:3 and 3:1 (for instance, 2 oz. carrot to 6 oz. celery then 2 hours later, 2 oz. celery to 6 oz. carrot). Mix the juices together and sip slowly.

Golden Milk   *page 68*

Golden Milk is a traditional yogic remedy for sore joints and stiffness, which are commonly experienced during detoxification and rehabilitation. It also rebuilds nerves.

- Drink 3 cups throughout the day for 40 days.

A delicious energizing, cleansing and nourishing drink. Yogi Tea is a daily staple of the regimen since its primary benefit is to strengthen the overtaxed liver. It is a blood purifier and has beneficial toning effects on the nervous, digestive and circulatory systems.

- First thing in the morning, drink a cold 8 oz. cup with no milk or sweetener. 3 to 5 times a day drink a hot or cold 8 oz. cup; add sweetener and milk to taste.

Supplements

Nutritional supplements help increase nerve strength that is depleted from stress and substance abuse.

Vitamin B complex or Super B with B6 and Pantothenic Acid

A lack of thiamine, one of the B vitamins most commonly missing, can lead to serious mental disturbances. Also, B vitamins strengthen the weakened nervous system and are important for protein metabolism.

- 100 mg twice daily.

- Recommended foods: fresh fruits and vegetables (preferably organic), rice bran syrup, brewer's yeast.

Vitamins A, C and E

Protein supplementation for vegetarians (we recommend 40 grams daily for women, 50 grams daily for men, and 60 grams for those who are physically active) will help reduce cravings and maintain emotional balance. it is Important for protection from infections and for healthy blood vessels.

- Vitamin A: at least 7500 I.U. per day.

- Vitamin C with bioflavonoids: 500 mg every 4 hours or 1000 mg per day.

- Vitamin E: 400–800 I.U. daily.

Additional Tips

Recommended foods: Oranges, broccoli, grapefruit, potatoes, tomatoes, strawberries, wheat germ oil, almonds, hazelnuts and peanuts.

- It is also important to take in plenty of amino acids, which help nourish the brain and promote nerve cell function and transmission of nerve impulses. Many abusive behaviors can result from low levels of amino acids. Supplementing amino acids can be of great help in recovery from addictions.

NICOTINE

Physiological Impact of Nicotine

Nicotine in the lungs is immediately absorbed into the blood.

In eight seconds, nicotine reaches the brain and the heart rate increases.

In 40 minutes the effects are diminished and a craving arises for more cigarettes.

More nicotine is required to maintain high levels of dopamine ("the feel good" neurotransmitters in the brain), otherwise the smoker feels irritable and depressed.

Nicotine selectively degenerates regions of the brain dealing with emotional control, making it highly addictive.

Nicotine Usage

20% of the U.S. population uses cigarettes, of which about 15% are teens.

87% of lung cancers can be directly linked to habitual smoking.

50% of smokers die from smoking-related illnesses.

Women who smoke while pregnant have a lower birthrate and their children may have significant health issues.

480,000 premature deaths each year are attributed to smoking.

SuperHealth® Perspective on Nicotine

Nicotine weakens the nervous system and depletes vitality and stamina. It diminishes neurotransmitters in the brain that affect the ability to be thorough. It also prevents the chemical reactions that cause messages to pass from one part of the brain to the other.

Nicotine replaces oxygen cells in the bloodstream, causing toxic build-up and reducing the capacity of the lungs to inhale oxygen, the essential ingredient of life.

Other Harmful Effects of Nicotine

- Creates an addictive mind-set.

- Often accompanied by depression.

- Under stress, the breath tends to become shallow. While nicotine may temporarily satisfy the need for a good deep breath, in the long run smoking only further depletes the oxygen supply.

- Can greatly diminish a person's ability to exercise patience.

- The loss of vitality makes one more vulnerable, easily influenced and taken advantage of.

- Impedes the fortitude necessary for follow-through and dependability.

SuperHealth® Technology to Promote Healing from the Effects of Nicotine

See pages 52-63 for pose instructions.

One may choose to practice any of these recommended breaths at any time to assist in relieving the "urge."

Using the Breath to Relieve Urges

Every time the urge to smoke arises use this breath control technique. It can be used for nicotine cravings or any other urge impulse.

Inhale 5 seconds deeply through the nose, hold the breath comfortably for 5 seconds and then slowly exhale the breath for 5 seconds. Do this breath at least 7–8 times whenever the urge arises. Practice throughout the day as many as 20 to 25 times with each urge.

Breath of Fire   *page 55*

This is one of the most powerful and cleansing breaths in Kundalini Yoga. It increases lung capacity, strengthens the nervous system, and also reduces addictive impulses for drugs, smoking and other compulsive behaviors.

Breath of Fire is a powerful blood cleanser. Acids are stored in the blood and the sudden increase of oxygen through Breath of Fire will cause them to break down. If one experiences sensations of dizziness with this exercise, stop or slow down. Always drink water after doing any yoga to flush toxins built up by substances.

This breath brings cooling energy to the body. It soothes "hot" emotions and supports a neutral and calm response to reactive and explosive situations.

Therapeutic Nutritional Formulas

See pages 66-76 for recipes.

Suggested Use of Plums, Prunes and other 'P' Fruits

These foods help cleanse the body of nicotine. Plums are a blood purifier and also beneficial to brain health. Take up to 10 plums a day which are best eaten in the afternoon.

Prune Drink

- Suggested use: Soak 6 prunes overnight in water. In the morning eat the prunes and drink the water. Prunes are a diuretic and help eliminate nicotine toxins from the bloodstream.

Eat other 'P' fruits: All fruits that begin with the letter 'P', such as pomegranate, peach, pineapple, persimmon, etc. are good for detoxification.

Raisins

They contain fructose and potassium.

High in iron, raisins have a unique faculty of affecting the brain cells quickly. They also help eliminate stress and depression. Eat at least a handful as needed to reduce or eliminate cravings.

The best way to chew raisins is to crush them under your teeth, paste them on your upper palate and then suck on them. This technique will affect your brain cells quickly.

Black Licorice Stick

It helps balance blood sugar and also reduces nicotine cravings. Chew often during the day.

Juices and Supplements

See pages 66-76 for recipes.

Pineapple Juice   *page 72*

Acts as an energizer.

- Suggested use: Drink one 8 oz. glass 1 to 2 times daily.

Beet, Carrot and Celery Juice

Celery is known to strengthen the nervous system and is a relaxer.

Beets are known as a blood purifier and help detoxify the liver.

Carrots are rich in beta-carotene, which is converted into vitamin A. This vitamin assists in flushing out toxins from the body and reduces bile and fat in the liver. The fiber in carrots help clean the colon and promote elimination.

- Suggested use: To begin, prepare no more than 3 oz. beet juice, 3 oz. carrot and 3 oz. celery juice. Mix together and add water to taste. Drink up to 3 glasses daily. Sip slowly. You can make more or less juice, but keep the ratio of each vegetable juice in equal parts.

Licorice Tea

For liver, kidneys and lungs.

- Suggested use: small handful licorice root per cup of water, 4 cups a day.

For cleansing the liver and purifying the blood.

- First thing in the morning, take 8 oz. cold (no milk or sweetener) to cleanse the liver.

- Suggested use: Drink hot or cold 8 oz. 3–5 x daily. Add sweetener and milk to taste.

- Recommended sweetener: honey, stevia, agave.

Vitamin B complex

A lack of thiamine, one of the B vitamins most commonly missing fromt the diet, can lead to serious mental disturbance. Vitamin B strengthens the weakened nervous system and is important for protein metabolism.

- B complex: 100 mg twice daily (containing 150 mg B6 in total).

- B5 Pantothenic acid: 500 mg twice daily.

- Recommended Foods: Fresh fruits and vegetables, preferably organic.

Vitamin C with bioflavonoids

Important for protection from infections and for healthy blood vessels.

- 500 mg every 4 hours or 1000 mg per day.

- Recommended Foods: Oranges, broccoli, grapefruit, potatoes, tomatoes, strawberries, citrus fruits, strawberries, blueberries, raspberries, watermelon.

Additional Tips

Eat lightly

As the metabolism is dramatically changing and the body experiences low metabolism it is important to eat lightly. This will help food digest properly during this sensitive time.

Drink Water

To expedite the elimination of toxins from the body, drink 8 glasses of water with a slice of lemon throughout the day; work up to 2 liters a day. Use a straw to protect tooth enamel.

Eat lots of Fresh Fruits and Vegetables

For improved digestion, assimilation and elimination, eat a lot of fresh fruits and vegetables, preferably organic, throughout the day.

Exercise

To expedite the cleansing process of eliminating toxins, it is a must to sweat. Work up to walking at least 3 miles a day or do some type of exercise for 1 hour daily for 40 days. Sauna, jacuzzi and massages are great. Go slowly and at your own pace. Don't overdo with fanaticism—pace yourself and be gentle with yourself.

General Nutrition Tips

- Avoid too much fat, especially saturated fat.
- Eat foods with adequate fiber (40–60 grams) and starch.
- Try to minimize eating processed sugar. Preferably use stevia, agave, honey or maple syrup.
- Avoid too much salt.
- Avoid excessive use of caffeine-containing beverages.

General Tips for Good Health

Work with your medical doctor or dietician to establish your particular requirements. In order to assure that the diet will provide optimal nutrition during the detoxification and rehabilitation process, the following are some general recommendations:

- Maintain ideal body weight.

- Eat at least 3 times a day.

- Eat a variety of foods. No single food provides all essential nutrients.

Unless you have other dietary guidelines, it is recommended to include daily a minimum of:

- Two servings of milk or milk products such as cheese, yogurt, or cottage cheese.

- Two servings of protein sources such as dried beans and peas. For vegetarians, women need 40 grams of protein daily, men 50 grams. If you are very physically active, aim for 60 grams.

- Four servings of fruits and vegetables including dark leafy greens and one citrus fruit daily, organic if possible.

- Four servings of unprocessed whole grains such as bread, cereals, rice and pasta.

- Avoid excessive intake of high-calorie, nutrient-poor foods such as sweets, cake, soda and fats.

Please consider this healthy food regimen to cleanse the system, balance the blood chemistry and enhance metabolism. It is in this condition that the hormones, neurotransmitters and brain chemistry are regulated, enabling a non-reactive, less emotional and more neutral state of mind.

In this neutrality, you will be less prone to the triggers of stress, depression, anxiety and fatigue, which will further aid in curbing the desire for an addictive substance.

MARIJUANA

Medical Marijuana:

The information in this book does not address the use of medical marijuana as a therapeutic remedy. Like other drugs that are used for proven purposes such as pain medications, the medical use of marijuana is a personal decision to be respected.

In this book however we will address the recreational use of marijuana with its associated risks and benefits that must be considered. Its use can become a dependency and has some consequences that can cause long term damage.

Impact of Marijuana on the Body and Mind

THC, or tetrahydrocannabinol, is the chemical responsible for marijuana's psychological and physiological effects, which include:

- Increased stress on the central nervous system, brain and pituitary gland.

- Clogs nerve synapses; slowing and impairing transfer of critical information.

- Causes brain to stop producing chemicals needed to "feel good."

- Damages the network of glands, organs and hormones involved in growth and development.

- Causes significant damage to air sacs of lungs, reducing oxygen consumption.

- May cause chemical addiction.

THC also affects parts of brain that govern:

- Emotions, memory, judgment, perception
- Mental focus, balance, and self-control
- Motivation, mood, anxiety, depression

Other Effects:

- Damages the reproductive system
- Increases chance of throat cancer
- Depresses the functioning of the immune system
- Increases blood pressure and heart rate
- Increases feelings of paranoia and panic

Groups of cannabinoid receptors affect mental and physical activities:

- Cerebellum – (Coordination)
- Hippocampus – (Short-term memory)
- Basal Ganglia – (Unconscious muscle movement and motor coordination)

SuperHealth® Perspective on Marijuana

Marijuana can be one of the most damaging drugs. It stimulates the brain and makes the user feel idealistic. The user becomes absent-minded and finds it difficult to relate to worldly responsibilities. Daydreams become stronger than real life activity.

Physiological Effects

Brain and nerve cells are nourished by cerebrospinal fluid. Healthy cerebrospinal fluid is rich in nutrients ("ojas") for the nervous system. Ojas is an ayurvedic term meaning vigor. Under the influence of marijuana, cells over-use and deplete ojas in the cerebrospinal fluid. The depletion of ojas leads to a *drought effect*, a deficiency of nutrients that causes brain cells to die off. This produces short term memory loss and decreased motivation.

Marijuana causes the mind to open and experience expansion. However, the expansion is unnatural.

The most significant impact occurs at the base of the brain where memory function is located. The storage of toxins in this area specifically contributes to short-term memory loss.

Marijuana causes a fundamental duality within the mind, body and spirit. The mind races quickly and experiences a false sense of expansion. This contributes to an imbalance in the highly sensitive nervous system, causing a split, which in turn creates irritability. A user may feel prickly, restless and anxiety-stricken. To relieve this discomfort, more marijuana is needed to take the edge off.

Marijuana interferes with the nerve activity in the spine and can lead to the loss of gray matter in the brain. Gray matter is the major component of the central nervous system that processes information originating in the sensory organs. As a result, balance, directional awareness and pain sensitivity are adversely affected.

Smoking any substance significantly damages the lungs, throat and esophagus.

Kundalini Yoga Exercises & Meditations to Promote Healing from the Effects of Marijuana

See pages 52-63 for pose instructions.

How Kundalini Yoga Helps

Marijuana gets stored in the upper back and the base of the neck. When there is an accumulation of toxins in one central location, this build-up creates a blockage. In this case, short-term memory is affected. A user is prone to daydream and fantasize. Worldly responsibilities are challenging since non-reality becomes more fulfilling than actual life experience.

The **Maha Agni Kriya** (page 59) puts a gentle pressure on the back of the lower neck area and releases the substance blockage into the bloodstream. Through the breath technique there is increased oxygen and circulatory functioning, so marijuana is eliminated from the bloodstream. Coupled with highly nutritious and delicious foods, the cleansing and rebuilding process is expedited.

Breath of Fire   page 55

Breath of Fire regulates the pituitary, the master gland. This affects the entire glandular system, which boosts the nervous system and enables the blood to rebuild itself.

Begin with 3 minutes and build up to 31 minutes every day.

Therapeutic Nutritional Formulas

See pages 66-75 for recipes.

These potent formulas cleanse the body, stimulate the endocrine system and help to heal damage to the nerves. By building up the body's reserves through minerals, vitamins and improved nutritional value of food, they also:

- provide a direct psychological impact.
- clear the mind in the development of inner direction and self-reliance.

This in turn supports the process of change, healing and a refined process of mental, spiritual, and physical detoxification in a unified state of consolidation and harmony.

Beet & Apple Juice

Beets are the color of blood and they are a blood purifier. Apples support the reduction of stress.

- Mix 1/4 oz. beet juice, 6 oz. apple juice. Recommendation: Add 4 oz. water to dilute the sweetness. Must sip slowly.

- Note: Beet juice should always be mixed with other juices because it is so cleansing. Never drink any amount of straight beet juice. Add water to taste.

Basil and Fennel Tea

This herbal combination strengthens the nervous system and has a cooling effect. Basil is soothing, with cleansing qualities. Fennel expels mucus, relieves muscle cramps and aids digestion.

- Boil 8 oz. of water, add a small handful of each herb and steep for 20 minutes as a tea. Drink one cup up to 3 times a day.

Banana Monofast Diet

This is an excellent recipe to eliminate the residue of THC from the brain. This is an extreme diet so be careful and sensitive to your capability. Please be flexible and do not get fanatical with your program.

Start this fast on the day of the new moon and continue for 14 days until the full moon. It is intended to build up worn tissues and adjust the iron and potassium factors in the body, removing sodium and replacing calcium.

- Breakfast: Drink 1 cup freshly squeezed orange juice with the pulp, sweetened with honey. After 1 hour eat 3 bananas. Chew thoroughly and eat the white strings inside the peel. Follow immediately by chewing the contents of one whole cardamom pod (seeds only) to aid the digestion of the bananas.

- Lunch: Eat 3 bananas followed by the seeds of one whole cardamom pod.

- Dinner: Eat 3 bananas followed by the seeds of a whole cardamom pod. If you feel weak, take more orange juice and honey during the day. For constipation, increase the cardamom pods to 3 at a time. Drink large amounts of pure, hot water and Yogi Tea (page 70).

Note: If you feel overly emotional or have a severe reaction to the diet at any time, break the fast. On the 15th day of the fast, drink only lemon juice, warm water and honey. Then for the next 28 days go on the **Mung Beans and Rice** diet (page 73).

COCAINE

Impact of Cocaine on the Body and Mind

Cocaine is a devastating drug, as addictive as any other known drug.

- Inhaling, the vapor immediately enters the bloodstream through the lungs.

- Users go on "runs," consuming as much as possible until they collapse from exhaustion.

- Users are constantly in search of the first-time high, but it's never again as good.

- In some places the monetary cost may be relatively low, but since experience of the high is so short, the use is very frequent. Therefore, there may be an increase in criminal activity to support the habit.

Impact of cocaine:

- Cocaine acts directly on the brain.

- Inhaled, it reaches the brain within 10 – 15 seconds.

- However, the high lasts only 5 to 15 minutes.

Side Effects:

As cocaine moves through the bloodstream, it first leaves the user feeling energized, alert and sensitive to sight, sound and touch, causing a "high" or "rush."

- Heart rate increases
- Pupils dilate
- Blood pressure and body temperature rise
- Soon thereafter, feelings of restlessness, anxiety or irritability may occur

Cocaine can lead to an increased risk of heart attacks, strokes and respiratory problems. Larger doses may lead to aggressive behavior, paranoia and delusions. Use may eventually result in severe mental disorders.

SuperHealth® Perspective on Cocaine

- Cocaine can lead to paranoia, where the user is excessively afraid, phobic and fearful.

- It can seriously affect the pituitary with as little as one use—also called a *drunken pituitary,* causing a desensitivity to life.

- "Blown out" pituitary can make a user feel stuck and can reduce him or her to a base physical and earthly existence with a limited sense of self.

- One loses the ability to "read between the lines" and understand the sentiment of the unspoken word from another person. This may create a loss of awareness of the subtleties of life.

- It interferes with the mental ability to communicate with sensitivity and at a higher frequency. Diplomacy, tact and intuition are diminished.

Kundalini Yoga Exercises & Meditations to Promote Healing from the Effects of Cocaine

See pages 52-63 for pose instructions.

Meditation to Help Break the Cocaine Habit   page 61

The use of cocaine artificially "revs" up the sympathetic nervous system and often makes it very difficult to rest and relax at will. This kriya balances the nervous system and acts as a check on the parasympathetic nervous system enabling a calming and peace-inducing effect on the body and mind.

This technology is so effective that in a controlled and supportive setting it can help to alleviate uncomfortable symptoms when reducing or limiting use of the drug.

Therapeutic Nutritional Formulas

See pages 66-74 for recipes.

Dark Leafy Greens

For restoring and nourishing a depleted system, eat a lot of dark leafy green vegetables, either sautéed, steamed or raw.

- Suggested serving: Minimum one time a day, up to 3 meals a day.

Carrot Juice

An excellent cleanse and delicious fresh and organic juice

- Suggested use: 8 ounces 3 times a day.

Vitamin C (with bioflavonoids)

Important for protection from infections and for healthy blood vessels

- 1000 mg per day.

- Recommended foods: Oranges, broccoli, grapefruit, potatoes, tomatoes, strawberries.

Vitamin E

- 400 – 800 I.U. daily.

KUNDALINI YOGA

Breath, Postures & Meditations

Kundalini Yoga Benefits and Helpful Tips

The breathing techniques, meditations and nutritional formulas in this book assist in expeditiously cleansing and rebuilding bodily systems. They create a state of mental clarity and heighten awareness with a sense of inner connectedness and personal fulfillment.

Happiness is proportionate to your rate and length of breath. The amount of oxygen you intake is proportional to your strength.

Water, water, water. Drink more and more!!!! Water helps to regulate mood swings, curb emotional reactions and assist in elimination and inner cleansing of the body.

During the three-day detoxification eat lightly to expedite toxin elimination from the body. A person may experience low stamina during this time. It is recommended to eat foods with less protein since it requires more energy to digest. This supports a person during this low energy phase.

Recommendations to follow as realistically as possible: vegetarian diet with fresh fruits and vegetables, either raw, steamed or sautéed, preferably organic.

Drink juices throughout the day. Reduce or eliminate caffeine, sugar, processed bread or oils.

During rehabilitation phase from four to forty days, add a variety of other fruits and vegetables with protein sources of cottage cheese or hard cheese, tofu, nuts, legumes and whole wheat bread. Try to reduce meat, fish and eggs, which require more digestive energy.

After forty days, follow good dietary measures: develop healthy eating habits, chew food well, and sit down when eating. An attitude of gratitude toward our food is the highest consciousness.

Sat Kriya

Maintain a daily yoga and meditation practice. **Sat Kriya** transmits energy up the spine. This kriya will help you control your emotions and nervous system strength.

You may experience low stamina at first so be sensitive and tune into yourself. Go slowly, but keep going. Practice at your own pace.

Please visit www.kri.org for beginning sets and full explanations of various yogic postures and terminology.

Visit http://www.3ho.org under IKYTA (International Kundalini Yoga Teachers Association) for an international yoga center directory.

Breathing Techniques

Long Deep Breathing

Instructions:

- Sit with spine straight in a chair or cross-legged. Hands are relaxed and resting on the knees.
- Close the eyes and focus at the point between the eyebrows.
- Take a deep full breath inhaling through the nose. Hold the breath, pulling the chest forward.
- Slowly exhale through the nose.
- Upon conclusion, inhale deeply and stretch arms over the head while pulling up the spine.
- Exhale and relax.

Benefits:

- Increase lung capacity and oxygen intake. Lack of oxygen in the blood contributes to depression, anxiety and other mental disturbances.
- Reduces toxic build-up in the lungs.
- Regulates the pH (acid/alkalinity) of the blood, helping it to detoxify.
- Pumps the spinal fluid to the brain, feeding it with nutrients.
- Promotes a calming and relaxing effect on the body and a peaceful state of mind.

Breath of Fire

Instructions:

- Sit with spine straight in a chair or cross-legged on the floor. Hands are either in your lap or you may start with one hand resting lightly over the navel and the other hand resting on your knee.

- To begin, pant like a dog with the mouth slightly open, keeping your tongue in your mouth. On the inhalation, the navel will automatically push out, while on the exhalation, the navel will automatically be pulled in. The focus of the energy is at the navel point.

- When you feel comfortable, close your mouth and bring both hands to rest on the knees as you continue to breathe powerfully and rapidly through the nose. The navel will automatically pump in and out. The inhalation and exhalation are equal in strength and length.

- Relax the face muscles as you continue the Breath of Fire.

- To end, inhale deeply and hold the breath in as you energize your entire body. Exhale and relax.

- Practice for 11 minutes each session three times a day. Be kind to yourself and when necessary, work up to this slowly and gradually.

Breath of Fire (Con't)

Benefits:

- One of the most powerful breaths in Kundalini Yoga.

- Increases lung capacity and strengthens the nervous system which has been weakened through substance use.

- Reduces addictive impulses for drugs, smoking and other compulsive behaviors.

- Powerful blood cleanser. If sensations of dizziness occur, slow down. Remember to always drink water after doing yoga to eliminate toxins from the body.

Sitali Pranayam

Instructions:

- Sit with spine straight in a chair or sit cross-legged on the floor.

- Curl the tongue length-wise, slowly inhale through the curled tongue; hold the breath a few seconds. Slowly exhale through the nose.

Benefits:

- Helps repair the imbalances in the nervous system from the use of substances. Works on the spine which is important since all nerves begin and end with the spine.

- Cooling breath. Activates the thyroid and parathyroid glands, helping boost the immune system and overcome illness.

- Brings the mind to a quiet, still point. Brings power, strength and vitality.

- As the physical body comes into balance, one has the reserve energy to deal with emotional or mental trauma which may have initiated the harmful habit or addiction.

Sitali Pranayam

Cow Pose

Kundalini Yoga Postures

Cow Pose Pumps

Instructions:

- Come onto the hands and knees. The hands are shoulder-width apart; knees are about 12 inches apart.

- Head stays up.

- Start pumping the navel in and out. The pumping action will normalize the breath.

- Begin with 1 minute a day and build up to 3 minutes.

Benefits:

- Restores nerve centers damaged by drugs or other substances.

- Pumping the navel helps with digestion.

- Pressure at the neck will slowly release toxic build-up. As the function of the circulatory system improves, substances move through and are eliminated out of the physical body system.

Kundalini Yoga Meditations

Maha Agni Pranayam for Marijuana Detoxification

Instructions:

- Sit in Easy Pose, Lotus Pose or in a chair, feet on the ground and spine straight. The focus during this meditation is to maintain a very stiff Neck Lock (see glossary) throughout the meditation.

- Place the palms flat together 9 – 12 inches in front of the chest at heart level.

- Inhale completely as you turn your head to your right shoulder and swing it across the chest to the left shoulder.

- Complete the swing by applying Neck Lock, while facing straight forward.

- Focus at the third-eye point and project this mantra silently, in perfect rhythm:

  Ra-Ra-Ra-Ra, Ma-Ma-Ma-Ma
  Ra-Ra-Ra-Ra, Ma-Ma-Ma-Ma
  Sa-Ta-Na-Ma

- Exhale and immediately swing the head again as you inhale. The head swing should be quick and should give a little pull at the base of the skull.

Maha Agni Pranayam

Maha Agni Pranayam for Marijuana Detoxification (con't)

Benefits:

- Maha Agni Pranayam is excellent for relieving the pressure that gathers at the base of the skull. Marijuana causes a blockage of spinal fluid at the meridians at the base of the neck, which can increase pressure. Pressure in this location blocks a small area related to memory (particularly short-term memory) and motivation. Doing this meditation can open that block and restore much of the memory function.

Meditation to Help Break the Cocaine Habit

Instructions:

- Sit with arms bent up and to the sides, hands in Gian Mudra (see glossary). Press shoulder blades together hard. Eyes closed.

- Begin by slowly taking a full 5 seconds to inhale, then hold the breath for 5 seconds and take a full 5 seconds to exhale. Repeat twice. Over time, gradually increase to 10 second sets. Remember to keep the inhale, hold and exhale the same length. Gradually work up to 15 or 20 second sets.

- Relax the breath and posture and breathe normally for 2–3 minutes.

- Resume posture. Inhale, press tongue with all strength against the roof of your mouth. Apply the Root Lock (see glossary) for 30 seconds. Exhale. Breath of Fire for 15 to 20 seconds. Repeat.

- Inhale. Press the tongue against the roof of the mouth for one minute. Exhale and relax.

Benefits:

- This kriya (see glossary) balances the nervous system and acts as a check on the parasympathetic nervous system. In a controlled, therapeutic setting this technology can be applied to alleviate uncomfortable symptoms.

Habituation Meditation

Instructions:

- Sit with spine straight in a chair or cross-legged.

- Make hands into fists, pressing the thumbs on the indentations of the temples.

- Lock the back molars together with closed mouth.

- Focus the eyes between the eyebrows.

- Breathe normally with a relaxed breath.

- Silently repeat: "Sa, Ta, Na, Ma". On each sound, vibrate the jaw muscles by pressing molars together and releasing. As you press together, you will feel a movement at your temples.

- To end, inhale and hold the breath for a few seconds exhale and relax.

- Practice 5–7 minutes. Gradually increase to 20 minutes and then to 31 minutes. Build up over 40 consecutive days.

Benefits:

- The pressure of the thumbs on the temples triggers a reflex in the brain, activating the pineal gland. This corrects an imbalance related to the persistence of addictions.

- This is one of the best meditations for drug dependence or any dependence and specifically benefits the rebuilding process during the rehabilitation phase.

Recipes

and Nutritional Formulas

Garlic, Onions and Ginger—The Trinity Roots!

Eat garlic, onions and ginger for increased energy and sustained health.

Cooking tip:

- Sauté one onion, a tablespoon of fresh grated ginger root and two cloves of garlic in a small amount of ghee (see opposite) or light vegetable oil until the onion becomes clear and soft.

- Add your favorite vegetables and spices. Continue cooking until the vegetables are tender.

Ghee

Ghee is healthier than butter and provides excellent internal lubrication. It provides a healthy and nutritious fat and is excellent for vitality and maintaining youth.

To make ghee:

- Melt a pound of butter in a heavy sauce pan (to prevent burning) and simmer slowly for about 30 minutes. Do not stir or shake pan. Solids will sink to the bottom and turn dark. A white foamy substance will form on top and most of this foam will boil away. After 30 minutes, skim off any substance still remaining on top and carefully pour off the clear, golden liquid into your ghee container. Discard the dark solids at the bottom of the pan. Ghee is ideal to sauté or bake vegetables.

Golden Milk

You may experience stiffness or aches in your joints. If so, this delicious drink is for you. It brings flexibility to the joints and will make you feel rejuvenated and youthful.

Turmeric is a bright orange spice that can be found in a grocery or health food store. It is excellent for joint lubrication.

Ingredients:

¼ tsp. turmeric
¼ cup water
8 oz. milk
2 tbsp. raw almond oil
honey or sweetener to taste

Boil turmeric in water for 8 minutes until it forms a thick paste. Add milk and bring to a boil. As soon as it boils, remove from heat and add almond oil and sweetener.

Zest for Life Juice

    6 oz. carrot juice
    1 oz. beet juice
    1 oz. lemon
    1 oz. ginger

Prepare the juice ingredients one at a time in a juicer. Then mix together and sip slowly. Drink every 3 hours if you are feeling lethargic, inattentive or unresponsive. Increases your zest for life!

Yogi Tea

Yogi Tea is a blood purifier, energy booster and strengthens the liver. It is also good for digestion, the nervous system and bones. Prepare fresh ingredients or, for your convenience, go to your local health food store and find boxed, pre-made Classic Yogi Tea with single serving tea bags on the shelves.

Instructions to prepare one serving:

10 oz. water
3 whole cloves
4 whole green cardamom pods
4 black peppercorns
½ stick cinnamon
1 slice ginger root
¼ tsp. or 1 small bag of black tea
1 cup of milk

Combine spices and water in a pot and bring to a boil, then reduce heat and let simmer for 20 minutes.

Remove from heat and add black tea (optional), steeping for a couple of minutes. Add milk and bring to a boil. Remove from heat and strain. Serve with honey to taste.

Makes one large mug or two small servings of Yogi Tea.

Pineapple Juice

Pineapple juice is an energizer and is recommended when detoxifying from depressants or "downers." It's sweetness provides a natural source of energy and counteracts low stamina. When the liver or kidneys are overstressed, this juice can give them the boost they need. Because of its high chlorine content, pineapple juice can be used to purge the body of wastes by stimulating urination, which is especially beneficial during the cleansing process.

Suggested use: drink one 8 oz. glass 1 to 2 times daily.

Mung Beans and Rice

There are many variations of this basic recipe adding various vegetables and spices.

1 cup mung beans
9 cups water
4–6 cups chopped assorted vegetables
  (carrots, celery, zucchini)
1 cup basmati rice
basil and bay leaf, optional

Masala Ingredients:

1/3 cup ghee or oil
2 onions, chopped
1/3 cup minced ginger root
8–10 cloves garlic, minced
1 heaping tsp. turmeric
1/2 tsp. pepper
1 heaping tsp. garam masala
1 tsp. crushed red chiles (more or less to taste)
seeds of 5 cardamom pods
salt, tamari sauce or Braggs to taste

Mung Beans and Rice (Con't)

Sort through the beans on a cookie tray and discard any pebbles. Wash the mung beans in a strainer.

Bring the water, washed mung beans, basil and bay leaves to a boil. Boil over medium-high flame for 30–40 minutes until the beans are soft.

While waiting for mung beans to finish cooking, heat 1/3 cup oil in large frying pan. Add onions, ginger and garlic and sauté over medium-high flame until lightly browned. Add all spices except the salt, tamari or Braggs.

If the mixture sticks to the pan, add a little more water and stir.

Combine the masala mixture with the cooking mung beans.

Chop the vegetables into bite-size pieces and place in a separate bowl. Wash the rice thoroughly. Add the vegetables and rice at the same time to the cooking mung beans and masala.

Bring back to a boil over a medium-high flame. As soon as it boils, turn down, cover and stir every 5–7 minutes, keeping the pot covered.

Cook for 20–25 more minutes in total. Add tamari, Braggs or salt to taste after serving.

Glossary

Glossary of Terms

Amino Acids

Organic compounds that are important building blocks in the cells, tissues and muscles of the human body. Amino acids also play a necessary role in neurotransmission and biosynthesis. Because amino acids cannot be synthesized from various chemicals within the human body, they must be consumed from outside sources. Many abusive behaviors can result from low levels of amino acids. Supplementation can aid addiction recovery.

Vegetarian sources of essential amino acids include milk, cheese, vegetables, nuts, grains and beans.

Depression and Depressive Disorders

Clinically, a general diagnosis of depression is given when a number of very specific symptoms appear to be present for longer than a two-week period in any individual. The *Diagnostic and Statistical Manual of Mental Disorders* (DSM) currently lists several depressive disorders ranging in severity and symptomology.

A Yogic Perspective:

From a basic energetic and yogic perspective, the root of depression is unresolved sadness and anger. Finding healthy ways to face these feelings is essential to reestablishing balance after undergoing a traumatic event. Meditation and Kundalini Yoga can be a safe way to reconcile chemical imbalances in the right and left hemispheres of the brain. When the hemispheres are synchronized and sharing information, there is a possibility for new thoughts, new approaches, new resolutions and a new-found hope that problems can be resolved.

Eye Focus

During meditation it is often recommended to have a specific gazing point in order to enhance the meditative experience. Common focal points are:

- *Brow Point*—The center of the forehead stimulates the pituitary and the intuitive centers.

- *Tip of the Nose*—stimulates the pineal gland and the frontal lobe. This gaze is said to help create new pathways in the brain.

- *Chin*—has a cooling and calming effect.

- *Crown chakra*—also referred to as the tenth gate, gazing toward the crown of the head stimulates it to open and affects the pineal gland.

- *1/10th open*—a balancing and calming focus that increases the body's receptivity to the effects of meditation.

Gian Mudra

A common hand position used in meditation. It is formed by touching the tip of the index finger to the tip of the thumb. Its effect is knowledge, receptivity, balance, and expansion.

Kundalini Yoga

Known as the "yoga of awareness," Kundalini Yoga creates vitality in the body, balance in the mind, and openness to the spirit. Kundalini Yoga consists of exercise sets (kriyas), breathing exercises (pranayamas) and meditations which work on the whole body (nervous system, glands, mental faculties, chakras) to develop awareness, consciousness and spiritual strength.

Kundalini Yoga positively impacts addictive behavior and substance abuse and offers a technology for human consciousness that allows one to achieve their total creative potential.

Limbic System

The limbic system consists of the hippocampus, amygdala and the septum. Drug use has been shown to impair these sensitive centers that are responsible for healthy emotional and social processing.

Locks or Bandhs

Learning and developing the three body locks brings depth and effectiveness to Kundalini yoga practice. Applying a contraction of a particular area of the body will help clear blocks that impede the natural flow of energy.

Neck Lock—Jalandhar Bandh

This lock is applied throughout yoga exercises unless you are moving the head, as in neck rolls, or are otherwise instructed. Apply the neck lock during most pranayam practices, meditations and while chanting.

* Neck lock is a gentle movement of the chin towards the back of the neck. To apply, keep the head and neck in a straight line with the spine and slightly tense the muscles of the neck and throat while keeping the face relaxed.

Diaphragm Lock—Uddiyana Bandh

This lock brings clarity to the heart for greater kindness and compassion. It also brings fiery transformative energy to aid in digestion.

* To apply the diaphragm lock, sit comfortably with a straight spine and exhale completely, holding the breath out. Pull the navel point in towards the spine and hold for 10–20 seconds before gently releasing the abdomen and inhaling.

Root Lock—Mulbandh

A powerful contraction of muscles and stimulation of energies that helps to redirect sexuality into creativity and vitality. The root lock is often applied at the end of exercises and meditations to seal the healing and uplifting effects.

- Apply the root lock by contracting and lifting up on the anus and sex organs while simultaneously contracting and pulling the lower abdominals and navel point in towards the spine.

Ong Namo Guru Dev Namo - Tuning In

Ancient sounds to bring you to your inner wisdom. It is advised to chant this mantra three times before any Kundalini Yoga practice. Sit with the spine straight in a chair or cross-legged with the hands together at the heart center in prayer pose. Take a long, deep breath and repeat "Ong Namo Guru Dev Namo" in one breath If you need to, sip a little extra breath after "Ong Namo."

Pronunciation:

Ong: sounds like "Oh" with the "ng" sound on the end as in the word "song."

Namo: sounds like the "a" in the word "ma" and the "o" in the word "go."

Guru: sounds like "goo roo."

Dev: sounds like the name "Dave."

Parasympathetic nervous system

One of the three main divisions of the autonomic nervous system responsible for regulation of internal organs and glands. It is responsible for "rest-and-digest" activities such as salivation, tear production, urination, and digestion.

Prana

The generating force related to the inhale of the breath. Prana is the energy of growth, vitality, healing, rejuvenation, expansion, and action.

Prayer Pose

Palms are together and upright at the heart. Right hand is the positive polarity and left hand the negative. This has a calming, neutralizing effect on the body and helps to focus the mind.

Sat Nam

"Sat" is Truth. "Nam" is name or the identity of Truth. When used as a greeting it means "I greet and salute that reality and truth which is your soul." It is called the Bij Mantra.

Shabd

Sound, especially subtle sound imbued with consciousness. It is a property of consciousness itself. Meditation on shabd awakens awareness.

Sympathetic nervous system

One of the three main divisions of the autonomic nervous system responsible for regulation of internal organs and glands, the sympathetic nervous system is responsible for the "fight or flight" response.

Yogi

One who has attained a state of yoga (union) where polarities are mastered. One who practices the disciplines of yoga and has attained self-mastery.

References

Breath of Fire: The Aquarian Teacher, 4th Ed., KRI 2007, pp. 95, 328

Cow Pose Pumps: The instructions for this pose are from the personal notes of Mukta Kaur Khalsa, Ph.D. and were not reviewed by KRI. The Aquarian Teacher, 4th Ed., KRI 2007, p. 313

Long Deep Breathing: The Aquarian Teacher, 4th Ed., KRI 2007, p. 92

Maha Agni Pranayam: Sadhana Guidelines, 2nd Ed, p. 153 – Marijuana Brain

Meditation for Healing Addiction: The Aquarian Teacher, 4th Ed., KRI 2007, p. 435; and the instructions for this book are from the personal notes of Mukta Kaur Khalsa, Ph.D. and were not reviewed by KRI.

Parasympathetic Nervous System: Praana, Praanee, Pranayam, pp. 86-87 – the Cocaine Meditation

Sat Kriya: The Aquarian Teacher, 4th Ed., KRI 2007, p. 348

Sitali Pranayam: The Aquarian Teacher, 4th Ed., KRI 2007, p. 97

Connect with Kundalini Yoga!

To find a Kundalini Yoga class near you,
visit www.3HO.org

Find DVDs and Kundalini Yoga manuals from the
Kundalini Research Institute at
www.kri.org.

Contact SuperHealth®

SuperHealth®, Inc.
www.super-health.net
superhealth12@gmail.com
1A Ram Das Guru Place
Española, New Mexico 87532 USA
Director: Mukta Kaur Khalsa, Ph.D.

Find a SuperHealth® teacher near you:
www.super-health.net

SuperHealth® is a 501(c)(3) tax-exempt non-profit
organization.